About the Author

Before being appointed B.A.F. National Coach in 1981, Max Jones worked in the field of Physical Education and Recreation Management. In 1982 he took on the position of Chief Coach for Throws and in this capacity was Team Coach to the Great Britain team at European, World and Olympic Games as well as being Chief Coach for the England Commonwealth Games team at the 1986 and 1990 Games. In 1991 he was appointed as Chief Coach for the Great Britain Junior Team.

Contents

Photographs

Cover photo of Jacqueline McKernan by Mark Shearman.
Photosequences by the late Howard Payne.

HISTORICAL DEVELOPMENT

The discus throw is a skilful event which was a feature of the ancient Games (Myron's sculpture) and was then performed as a standing throw from a sloping platform.

At the time of the first modern Olympics in 1896 two versions existed: the ancient style and a 'freestyle', the latter won by Robert Garrett with 29.15m. Gradually there was a move away from the standing throw, taking advantage of the 'square' area provided for the throwing action. By 1912 the 'square' had evolved into a 2.50 metre circle.

Athletes seeking more speed developed a $1\frac{1}{2}$ turn action (Fig. 1) which initially was in the form of a pirouette around the left leg, with the thrower assuming a high throwing position. This style involved no loss of ground contact and was very much an 'arm' throw. By the 1930's the $1\frac{1}{2}$ turn style had progressed to a jump turn with the arm following a wave-like pattern. This basic $1\frac{1}{2}$ turn technique lasted until the early 1950's with the leading exponent being Consolini (Italy), the 1948 Olympic Champion (Fig. 2).

An obvious improvement in efficiency was for the thrower to turn his back to the

500 B.C. Discus Throw

direction of throw in his initial stance and therefore perform $1\frac{3}{4}$ turns. This type had been tried as early as 1900, but it was not until the post-war period that it became universally used and today this is still the basic technique.

A version of the one and three quarter turn technique was the 'falling balance' used by the American Bob Fitch (Fig. 3) and popularised by Fortune Gordien, the world record holder (59.28m in 1953), where the upper body was allowed to fall into the centre of the circle with the feet trying to catch up and create balance.

Fig. 1. Early 20th Century (1900–1930) $1\frac{1}{2}$ turn technique.

Fig. 2. Mid 20th Century (1940–50) Jump turn — Consolini (Italy).

Fig. 3. The 'Falling' $1\frac{3}{4}$ turn — Bob Fitch (U.S.A.) c. 1946.

Fig. 4. Jay Silvester (U.S.A.) — wide Swing-Kick action c. 1961.

Fig. 5.

Wolfgang Schmidt (Germany)
(PLATE 1).

Today the techniques used vary from extreme swing-kick styles to simple running rotations, with the majority of throwers falling between the two extremes.

Wolfgang Schmidt (Germany) is an example of how the best of previous 'styles' has been honed into a smooth dynamic movement that exemplifies modern discus throwing (plate 1).

Interesting minor technique variations have also been introduced from time to time. Melnik (USSR) used a heel-ball entry to execute a smoother initial movement, but with the consequence of losing circle space. This was very popular in the early seventies, but has since declined in usage. Many throwers have experimented with the discus held behind the back during the turn, Oerter (Fig. 6), four times Olympic Champion,

By the late fifties the dynamic jump-turn took hold and the diminutive Piatkowski (Poland) used it with great effect (world record 59.91m). The main defect of this style was that the inevitable 'give' on landing in the centre of the circle detracted from the continuity of the throw.

Realising the limitations of the jump-turn, there was a move to flatten out the jump and, aided by a swing-kick of the right leg on entry, Silvester (Fig. 4) took the world record through the 60 metre barrier, eventually achieving an unsanctioned 70 metre throw. This swing-kick form of turn found almost universal adoption amongst the female throwers. Westermann reached 60 metres in 1967 and Melnik reached 70 metres in 1975.

Largely through the success of Danek (world record 66.07m — 1966) and John Powell (69.08m world record — 1975), the running rotation (Fig. 5) using a controlled right leg movement became very successful.

Jurgen Schult (Germany), the 1988 Olympic Champion. (PLATE 2).

3

Fig. 6. Al Oerter (U.S.A.) — individual discus carry into the throwing position c. 1960.

being the most successful example. This is a style of throwing rather than a basic essential.

Many throwers throw from a fixed front foot position, believing that this is mechanically sound. The G.D.R. coaches advocated this style of throwing in the late sixties and early seventies. Jurgen Schult (Germany), the 1988 Olympic Champion, uses this technique to great effect. (Plate 2). The fixed feet delivery has great popularity amongst women throwers, whereas the majority of the men jump or reverse release due to explosive use of the legs in the throwing action.

Although many have attempted to take the one and three quarter turn further round to a full two turns, this has met with little success. The one and three quarter turn technique will probably remain the basic technique, although throwers will give their own style to the basic movement.

			Barrier Breakers			
1900	41.50	J. Kemppainen (Fin)	40 metres	40.35	J. Wajsowna (Pol)	1932
1912	47.58	J. Duncan (U.S.A.)	45 metres	45.53	G. Mauermayer (Ger)	1935
1930	51.03	E. Krenz (U.S.A.)	50 metres	50.50	N. Dumbadze (USSR)	1946
1948	55.33	A. Consolini (Ita)	55 metres	57.04	N. Dumbadze (USSR)	1952
1961	60.56	J. Silvester (U.S.A.)	60 metres	61.26	L. Westermann (FRG)	1967
1962	61.10	A. Oerter (U.S.A.)	200 ft.			
			(60.96m)	61.26	L. Westermann (FRG)	1967
1965	65.22	L. Danek (Cze)	65 metres	67.32	A. Menis (Rum)	1972
1976	70.24	M. Wilkins (U.S.A.)	70 metres	70.20	F. Melnik (USSR)	1975
			75 metres	76.80	G. Reinsch (Ger)	1988

BASIC MECHANICS OF THE DISCUS THROW

The sole object of competitive discus throwing is to throw the implement as far as possible away from the front rim of the 2.50 metre circle. Governing the distance thrown are *four* factors. In all throwing events three factors affect distance thrown (height of release, speed of release, angle of release) with a fourth factor, i.e. aerodynamics, being present in discus throwing.

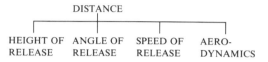

DISTANCE

| HEIGHT OF RELEASE | ANGLE OF RELEASE | SPEED OF RELEASE | AERO-DYNAMICS |

Height of Release

Assuming that the athlete has reasonable technique, there is little the coach can change since height of release is governed by the physical height of the athlete. All things being equal, the taller man will throw further, but the advantage is small in comparison with total distance thrown.

Angle of Release

The optimum angle for a projectile is 45 degrees, but this is calculated from ground level. The optimum angle of release for a discus is between 30 degrees and 40 degrees, with the longer throws generally having a lower angle of release. Ignoring the aerodynamic qualities of the discus, the varying angle of release itself would not produce radical changes in distances.

Speed of Release

The speed of release is governed by the force the athlete can generate and the effective range through which the athlete can apply this force. This is the most important factor since distance thrown is proportional to the square of the velocity, ie. if the velocity is doubled, the distance thrown will be quadrupled. The speed of release is increased according to the following equation:

$$\frac{\text{AVERAGE FORCE} \times \text{TIME OF APPLICATION}}{\text{MASS OF THE IMPLEMENT}}$$

The athlete can increase the 'average force' part of the equation by strength-training and technical synchronisation. The 'time of application' can be extended by improvements in technique and mobility. Although limited by the confines of a 2.50 metre circle, the athlete, using modern technique, can apply his force to the discus over a nine metre path. The acceleration of the discus is not uniform over the nine metres, the greatest acceleration occurring over the final double support phase immediately prior to release.

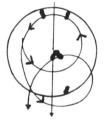

The Path of the Discus

Aerodynamics

Air resistance causes the discus to follow a flight curve that is not parabolic.

Many potentially long throws have been spoilt by the athlete not taking full advantage of the aerodynamic qualities of the discus. It has been stated that the angle of release should be somewhere between 30 degrees and 40 degrees, but it is important that the discus itself is tilted in such a way that it has a negative angle of 'attack', ie. its nose is kept down so that it is slightly below the line of the flight path (see diagram).

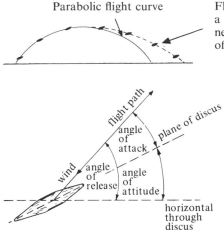

Parabolic flight curve

Flight curve of
a discus with a
negative angle
of attack

Diagram from
'The Science of
Track & Field
Athletics'

by H. & R. Payne.

This angle changes as gravity begins to slow the discus down. The last half of the discus flight is marked by a positive angle of attack and the discus experiences a pronounced lift.

The negative angle of attack in the early flight path is essential, since the gyrating of the discus (produced by the spinning of the discus at release) must not present a large surface area to the approaching air. As long as the discus is kept spinning, the surface area to the wind will be small. Eventually, however, even on a perfect throw, the spinning slows down and the near edge (to the thrower) of the discus will drop. This is caused by a large surface area being presented to the wind.

It is important for the athlete to understand the effects of wind upon his event. Since a headwind increases the velocity of air flow past the discus, its aerodynamic effects are very similar to an increase in velocity. Both lift and drag effect are made upon the disc but initially, on a well flighted discus, lift is predominant and therefore a headwind is an advantage — ideally a right quartering headwind for a right-handed thrower. To take advantage of headwinds, the leading edge of the discus should be kept down.

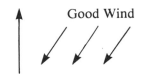

Good Wind

Direction of Throw

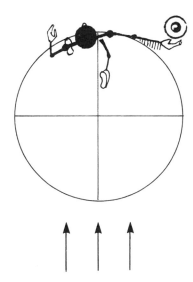

Negative Wind Condition

6

COMPETITION RULES FOR THROWING THE DISCUS

(a) In order to avoid accidents throwing sectors must be roped off at a height of approximately 1m and to make a 60° safety sector inside which the discus throwing sector is centrally placed. Alternatively, the central throwing area must be roped off as a unit at a height of 1 metre.

(b) Competitors must be given instructions that implements must be thrown during practice only from the circle. Implements must be returned by *hand* during practice or competition and must not be thrown back to the starting area. The Referee or other appropriate official shall disqualify from competing in the event any athletes who wilfully disobey the above instructions after having their attention drawn to them.

(c) No practice trials shall be allowed after a competition has begun.

(d) All throws shall be made from a cage.

(e) The competition may be decided in either of the following two ways—the conditions should, if possible, be printed in the programme and must be explained to the competitors before the competition begins.
   (i) Each competitor being allowed from three to six trials; or
   (ii) Each competitor being allowed three trials and the three to eight best competitors being allowed three more trials.

(f) Each competitor shall be credited with the best of all his trials.

(g) No competitor may place, or cause to be placed, any mark within the throwing sector.

(h) Competitors shall use only those implements provided for general use. Subject to any regulation laid down by the promoting body, a competitor who wishes to use his own implement must submit it to the Referee for approval and when it has been approved, it shall be available for the use of all competitors.

(i) Gloves may not be worn.

(j) No device of any kind, eg. taping of fingers, which in any way assists a competitor when making a throw shall be allowed.
Note: The use of tape to cover injuries to the hand will be allowed only if the Referee is saitsfied on medical or other evidence that the tape is necessary. The use of tape on the wrist will be allowed.

(k) (i) In order to obtain a better grip, competitors are permitted to use an adhesive substance on their hands only.
   (ii) In order to protect the spine from injury, a competitor may wear a belt of leather or some other suitable material.

(l) Competitors must not spray or spread any substance on the surface of a throwing circle nor on their shoes.

(m) Competitors must commence the throw from a stationary position within the circle; they may adopt any position they choose.

(n) It shall be a foul throw if the competitor, after stepping into the circle and starting to make the throw, touches with any part of the body the ground outside the circle, or the top of the circle rim. A competitor is allowed to touch the inside of the iron band.

(o) The competitor must not leave the circle until the discus has touched the ground. When leaving the circle the first contact with the top of the circle rim or the ground outside the circle must be completely behind the white line which is drawn outside the circle, the rear edge of which runs theoretically through the centre of the circle. (See diagram at top of next page).

(p) Provided that in the course of a trial the foregoing Rules have not been infringed,

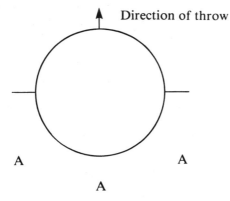

Direction of throw

NOTE: *To comply with this rule a competitor's first step on leaving the circle must be wholly in the area marked 'A'.*

A   A

A

To set out and to check sectors for Shot and Hammer and Discus.

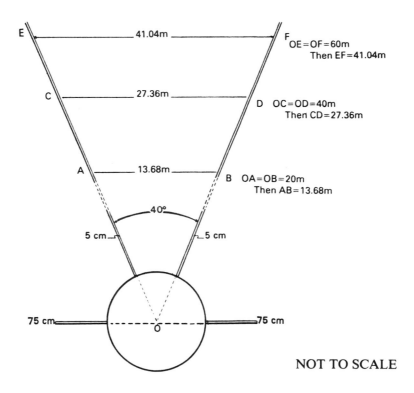

E   41.04m   F

OE=OF=60m
Then EF=41.04m

C   27.36m   D   OC=OD=40m
Then CD=27.36m

A   13.68m   B   OA=OB=20m
Then AB=13.68m

40°

5 cm   5 cm

75 cm   75 cm

O

NOT TO SCALE

NOTE. *The outer ends of the sector lines should be marked with flags.*

a competitor may interrupt a trial once started, may lay down the discus, may leave the circle before returning to a stationary position and beginning a fresh trial.

(q) A foul throw or letting go of the discus in an attempt shall be reckoned as a trial. If a discus breaks during a fair throw it shall not be counted as a trial.

(r) For a valid throw the discus must fall completely within the inner edges of lines marking a sector of 40° set out on the ground so that the radii lines cross at the centre of the circle.

NOTE: If a discus first hits the cage and then lands within the sector, the throw shall not, for that reason, be considered invalid.

NOTE: The 40° sector may be laid out accurately and conveniently by making the distance between two points on the inside edge of the sector lines 40m from the centre of the circle exactly 27.36m apart. The outer ends of the sector lines should be marked with flags.

(s) All measurements must be made from the nearer edge of the mark first made in the ground by the discus to the inner edge of the circle along a line drawn from the mark to the centre of the circle.

(t) A steel or fibre-glass tape should be used for measurement, and that part of the tape showing the distance thrown must be held by the official at the circle. Alternatively approved datum measurement equipment may be used, as may a scientific apparatus which has obtained a certificate of accuracy from a nationally recognised standardising organisation.

(u) The distance shall be recorded in even centimetre units to the nearest unit below the distance measured if that distance is not a whole even centimetre.

Throwing the Discus Specifications

(a) The circle shall be measured from the inside. The surface should be of concrete, asphalt, or some other firm but not slippery material. The surface should be lightly stippled when being laid to give a rough but not ribbed surface.

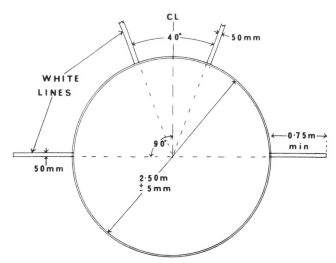

Layout of Discus Circle

(b) The surface of the inside of the circle should be level and 20mm ± 6mm lower than the upper edge of the ring which should be level with the ground outside.

(c) Circle rings:

Construction —
The rim shall be made of band iron, steel or other suitable material and be painted white.
Measurements —
(Metal) — The inside diameter of the circle shall measure 2.50m maximum and the rim of the circle shall be at least 6mm thick.
(Wood) — The inside diameter of the circle, shall measure 2.50m and the rim of the circle shall be 7.5cm thick.

A tolerance of ± 5mm is permitted for the inside diameter of the circle.

(d) A white line 5cm wide shall be drawn from the top of the circle, extending for at least 75cm on either side of the circle,

the theoretical extension of this line across the circle dividing it into front and rear halves with the rear edge passing through the centre of the circle.

(e) A portable circle meeting with the specifications above is permissible.

(f) The body of the discus shall be made of wood, or other suitable material, with a metal rim, the edge of which shall be circular. The cross-section of the edge shall be rounded in a true circle having a radius of approximately 6mm. Circular plates set flush into the side of the body and in the exact centre of the discus may be used to secure the weight. Both sides shall be identical and shall have no indentations, projecting points or sharp edges. The sides shall taper in a straight line from the beginning of the curve of the rim to a circle of a radius of 25mm to 28.5mm from the centre of the discus.

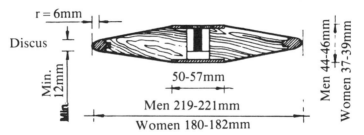

A discus can also be made of other materials without metal plates so long as the measurements and the weight correspond to the specifications.

The discus shall conform to the following specifications:

	WEIGHT	OUTER DIAM. OF METAL RIM		DIAM. OF METAL PLATES		THICKNESS AT CENTRE		THICKNESS OF RIM AT 6mm FROM THE EDGE
		Min	*Max*	*Min*	*Max*	*Min*	*Max*	
MEN SENIORS	2kg	219mm	221mm	50mm	57mm	44mm	46mm	12mm
JUNIORS	1.75kg	210mm	212mm	50mm	57mm	41mm	43mm	12mm
UNDER 17	1.5kg	200mm	205mm	50mm	57mm	37mm	42mm	12mm
UNDER 15	1.25kg	180mm	182mm	50mm	57mm	37mm	39mm	12mm
UNDER 13	1kg	180mm	182mm	50mm	57mm	37mm	39mm	12mm
WOMEN (all age groups except Under 13)	1kg	180mm	182mm	50mm	57mm	37mm	39mm	12mm
UNDER 13	0.75kg							
VETERANS Men 40–49	2kg	219mm	221mm	50mm	57mm	44mm	46mm	12mm
Men 50–59	1.5kg	200mm	205mm	50mm	57mm	37mm	42mm	12im
Men 60 and over	1kg	180mm	182mm	50mm	57mm	37mm	39mm	12mm
Women 35 and over	1kg	180mm	182mm	50mm	57mm	37mm	39mm	12mm

NOTE: It is recommended that implements issued for competition should exceed the specified weights by at least 5gm.

SAFETY IN THROWING

The discus event is a perfectly safe pastime that *can* be *lethal*. With common sense applied, no accident should occur. The following common sense rules should be adhered to:-

(1) When throwing in a group situation, the rule 'ALL THROW, ALL RETRIEVE' should be strictly adhered to.

(2) Throwing should only take place from the designated circle and the discus must *never* be thrown back to the circle.

(3) The athlete should always look towards the throwing area before throwing to ensure that it is safe to throw.

(4) The throwing area should be roped off, which deters other persons from crossing the area or at least makes them think.

(5) When operating without a cage, the coach must ensure that both he and other throwers stand well clear and to the rear of the circle.

(6) Ensure that the throwing circle is free from mud, stones etc.

ATHLETICS COACH

THE COACHING BULLETIN OF THE B.A.F.

Published:

March, June, September, December

Details from:

**Malcolm Arnold
56 Rolls Avenue
Penpedairheol
Hengoed, Mid. Glam. CF8 8HQ**

TECHNIQUE OF DISCUS THROWING

The following pages are devoted to a detailed analysis of discus throwing with the aid of sequence photographs. While this method of analysis is useful, it does not convey the feel, rhythm or continuity of the discus throw. A photograph represents one point in time and does not show what happened immediately before or immediately afterwards. No sequence conveys what the athlete was intending to do or the concept he was working to. The coach must spend many hours standing at the circle, observing throwers, in order to gain expertise in discus coaching. Articles, descriptions, analysis: these are only part of the learning process.

I have intentionally not devoted space to the teaching of the event since this is more than adequately covered in the B.A.F. books 'How to Teach the Throws' and 'But First'.

The Grip

No matter how efficient the technique, if the grip is incorrect the resulting distance will be disappointing due to poor flight. It is essential that the novice grips the discus correctly.

He can choose one of two grip variations:-
(a) The discus is held against the palm of the hand with the rim of the discus held on the first joints of the four fingers, so that the finger pads are turned over the rim. The fingers should be comfortably and evenly spaced (see below). The discus must not be tightly gripped, but held as relaxed as possible. The thumb is held flat across the discus and will give stability on release.

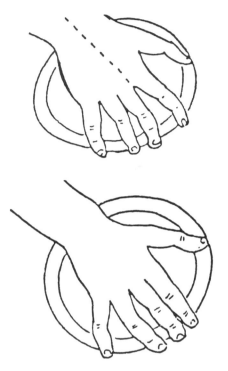

(b) As above, but with the first two fingers held together.

KEYS TO GOOD THROWING

Before taking a detailed look at the event it is worth considering the basic fundamentals that all good throwers will incorporate into their technique but often disguise by style. (All instructions in the text are given for right-handed throwers).

Rhythm

The whole throw must have rhythm — the same rhythm for every throw, for this will ensure the timing of the throw. To throw faster or harder the rhythm does not change. The rhythm can be counted thus: 1 – – – – 2 – – 3 with one (1) being the moment the left foot leaves the back of the circle, two (2) the moment the right foot lands in the middle of the circle and three (3) the moment the left foot lands at the front of the circle 1– – – –2– –3.

LR1

Balance

No matter how powerful the thrower, if balance is not present the throw will be a poor one. Balance must be achieved early at the back of the circle (LR2) if the all important throwing position is to be a balanced one.

LR2

Acceleration

The thrower must think of the concept of SLOW to FAST — finishing the throw fast, starting the throw slow. If the acceleration pattern of the throw were scientifically plotted, it would not show linear acceleration — but that should be the aim.

LEGS DOMINANT — The discus throw is dominated by the legs. The legs/feet dictate the speed, rhythm, direction and timing of the throw. If the leg action is correct, it will almost certainly follow that the whole throw will be correct.

LR3

Range

The thrower's force must be applied over as great a range as possible, taking into account the athlete's strength and mobility. Range can be judged at the moment the left foot is grounded at the front of the circle (LR 4).

LR4

Left Side Brace

The final throwing action must be performed against an erect, braced left side so that the right side of the body can work against it. The thrower should think of blocking the whole of the left side during the final throwing/flinging movement.

LR5

Relaxation

The discus must be thrown without tension — long throws cannot be forced. Long levers are relaxed levers.

LR6

Sequence — LARS RIEDEL (Germany) 1991 World Champion

Preliminary Swings

Aim: to establish the correct rhythm and balance for the entry into the turn.

The thrower takes up a position at the rear of the circle with the feet slightly wider than shoulder width apart. The swings should be performed in an easy, relaxed manner with the bodyweight being transferred rhythmically from right to left and vice versa. It is a mistake to make the swings too extensive and allow the bodyweight to transfer outside of the stance, since this will perhaps make it difficult for the athlete to obtain a balanced entry. To take the arm further back than is exhibited in S1 would be a mistake, and the athlete should think of restricting the amount of right hip turn allowed in the back swing.

Variations

At all levels of competition there are exhibited individual variations but the aim is always the same, ie. to enter 'on balance' with optimum speed.

Key Points

SIMPLE — RELAXED — WEIGHT TRANSFERENCE — RHYTHM

Sequence of WOLFGANG SCHMIDT (Germany), former world record holder and Olympic medallist.

| S1 | S2 | S3 |

Entry

Aim: a balanced position at optimum speed.

At the end of the preliminary swings the thrower must enter the turn on balance. The entry is initiated by the left knee (S4 & 5) to the left with the athlete adopting a shallow sitting position, the trunk held almost erect and the head in alignment. The bodyweight of the athlete is transferred over to the left side. Note that the left knee (S5) turns ahead of the shoulder axis.

On entry (S6) the bodyweight should be centred over the left foot. It is advantageous to think of the CHIN/KNEE/TOE being in vertical alignment upon entry. At this point it is essential to restrict the rotation of the left shoulder and there should be a feeling of holding it back during the entry phase. In order to slow down the shoulder axis, it is helpful if both the right and left arms are kept as wide as possible throughout the entry. The right hip should lead the body throughout the entry phase.

It is a mistake to hold the discus back at entry rather than let it trail the hip on a long relaxed arm. The right foot will leave the ground naturally on entry.

CHIN/KNEE/TOE

Key Points

BALANCE OVER LEFT LEG — HIPS LEAD SHOULDERS.

S4

S5

S6

Turn (or Run Across)

Aim: to gather horizontal and angular velocity and to land in an efficient throwing position.

Having obtained a balanced entry position (S6 & 7), the athlete must drive across the circle into a rangy power position (S11). The drive is a combination of propulsion from both the left and right legs. Some athletes prefer to make it left dominated (Powell 1.) and simply run across the circle, whilst others (Hellmann 1.) are right leg dominated, either swinging (S7-9) or kicking the right foot to the centre. Amongst the world elite there are many variations exhibited, and the athlete and coach must evolve a turn/run across that suits his/her physical type — there is no right or wrong way to progress across the circle.

Ideally the drive across the circle should be a combination of left and right power – the left giving linear drive and the right rotational speed.

Key Points

LEFT AND RIGHT LEG DRIVE — FOCAL POINT

POWELL 1

HELLMANN 1

S7

S8

S9

Many athletes use a focal point when driving across, looking at a point on the horizon at about the 10 to 12 o'clock area (see diagram). The use of a focal point helps with linear drive.

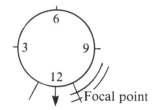

Power Position

Aim: a balanced, torqued position.

The athlete should arrive in a throwing position in a powerful, well balanced, torqued position (S10).

It is essential that the feet move quickly in the turn and ground in the correct position (Fig. 7). Not enough emphasis is placed upon the rhythm of the throw. The throwing rhythm in discus should be 1.........2..3, the 1 being the loss of left foot contact at the back of the circle, 2 — right foot contact in the middle, and 3 — left foot contact at the front. The quick 2..3 means that both feet are down quickly at the front and the final throw can begin. The athlete must work to achieve this rhythm.

The key feature in this phase is the position of the discus when the left leg grounds (S11) since it is only then that effective work can commence. Schmidt exhibits great range, not only with the throwing arm, but also in the lean of the body towards the rear of the circle. A late left foot will always result in loss of range.

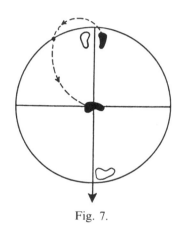

Fig. 7.

Note the position of the feet in S11 with the left foot slightly offset, the right toe being in line with the left heel, therefore allowing room for the hips to drive through.

Key Points

RHYTHM — FAST FEET — RANGE

S10

S11

The Throw (or Sling)

Aim: to give the discus as much velocity as possible.

It should be noted that the throw should be thought of as a continuous, flowing movement and that the final slinging action is not something performed in isolation. The moment the right foot makes contact with the circle (S10) it should continue the turning movement. It is a common error for the right foot to 'ground' and stop moving. The immediate turning of the right foot will cause the knee to turn, the hip to turn, the shoulder to turn and the arm to come through fast and relaxed.

The final throwing action can only effectively commence when the left foot is grounded (Powell 2) and therefore the left side of the body can act as a brace for the right side to accelerate around. The initial movement of the right leg/hip is rotational (S12) and it is a mistake to create too much lift at this point. During the initial throwing movement (S11-S12) the discus will naturally follow a downward path, but care should be taken to keep this to a minimum since 'scooping' the discus is a fault which will result in too high a throw and loss of distance. The athlete should try to keep the shoulders as level as possible throughout the throw, and especially so in the final flinging action.

POWELL 2

S12

S13

S14

The aim of any thrower is to keep the front foot down as long as possible (S13) whilst the right side drives forward. Many world class throwers, especially men, will lose ground contact before release due to the tremendous power of their legs. The concept of trying to maintain ground contact is a good one, whilst in reality it is difficult to achieve.

Many coaches place great emphasis upon the movement of the non-throwing arm, but care must be taken since too active a left arm movement may destroy the drive of the right side of the body in the final throwing action. It may be better to look upon the non-throwing arm as a counterbalance to the pulling effect of the centrifugal force on the throwing arm.

Variations

Many throwers, especially female, prefer to complete the throw over a fixed front foot. Mechanically this is good practice, since force can only be imparted whilst the athlete is in contact with the surface of the circle. It is a fact that the majority of world class male athletes develop so much power from the legs that they find it impossible to keep contact. As distances increase the fixed feet thrower will have to ensure that the lower back is well conditioned so as to avoid lower back injuries.

The majority of throwers reverse their feet at the end of the throw to remain in the circle (S14). A variation on the simple reverse is the Spin Release, with the athlete spinning around the front leg to stay in. Athletes using this variation must be careful not to cut short the throw and go into too early a spin — a common fault.

JURGEN SCHULT (Germany) who set the present (1993) world record of 74.08 in 1986 using the active reverse style of throwing. Subsequent to that throw he converted to fixed feet throwing, as above, and became competitively the best thrower in the world in the late eighties, winning the European, World and Olympic titles in the 1987/90 period. His best throw using fixed feet is 70.46.

THE THREE BASICS ILLUSTRATED

Martina Hellmann (Germany)
Olympic Champion

Wolfgang Schmidt (Germany)
European Champion
World Record Holder

BALANCE ON ENTRY

Jay Silvester (U.S.A.)
World Record Holder

Al Oerter (U.S.A.)
Olympic Champion
World Record Holder

John Powell (U.S.A.)
World Record Holder

Wolfgang Schmidt (Germany)
European Champion
World Record Holder

RANGE IN THE POWER POSITION

Martina Hellmann (Germany)
Olympic Champion

Mac Wilkins (U.S.A.)
Olympic Champion
World Record Holder

Martina Hellmann (Germany)
Olympic Champion

Wolfgang Schmidt (Germany)
European Champion
World Record Holder

LEFT SIDE BLOCK

Mac Wilkins (U.S.A.)
Olympic Champion
World Record Holder

Al Oerter (U.S.A.)
Olympic Champion
World Record Holder

SCHULT and MIKHALCHENKO — a comparison

"There are many ways to throw a long way". World ranking discus throwers will give their own individual interpretations to the basic technical model. Oerter is unlike Schmidt, who is unlike Schult; but they are all good throwers, applying their own individual style to the basic technique. The coach must be careful not to impose his particular style on to all his athletes. They will all have different qualities such as strength, mobility and different lever lengths and therefore no two throwers are ever the same.

The coach should also be aware of the variations between the men's and the women's events and these can be summarised as follows:-

(a) Women tend to be smaller than men (major games average — 1.80 as against 1.94 metres) and therefore the circle will be relatively larger for them, allowing much more freedom in the turn across the circle.

(b) The women's implement is fifty per cent lighter than the men's, and yet women will have approximately seventy per cent of the men's strength levels. The women's discus is therefore relatively lighter in ratio to strength levels. The women's discus can be 'man handled' into positions throughout the throw.

(c) Women on average tend to be more mobile, especially in the shoulder girdle, and can assume a more rangy power position. The power position is very crucial to women's throwing and the throw is less dependent upon the turn than is the men's.

(d) Men, who are relatively stronger in the legs, have greater difficulty in maintaining contact with the ground than do women at the end of the throw.

The following is an analysis and comparison of JURGEN SCHULT (Germany — Olympic, World and European Champion, World Record holder) and LARISA MIKHALCHENKO (Ukraine — major games medallist).

Both exhibit very similar positions in photos 1 & 2. Note that Mikhalchenko has placed the left foot off the back rim of the circle which will make the entry easier. At 1.80 tall she can afford to do this, whilst Schult at 1.93 cannot afford such extravagance.

Mikhalchenko, as with many world class women, exhibits a flamboyant back of the circle form but achieves the objective of the entry — balance. Schult is careful to control the left side of the torso and arm on entry, ensuring that the hips lead the shoulders.

Schult shows a controlled use of the right leg, with the left contributing to a linear drive across the circle. Mikhalchenko's right leg action (M4-M6) is the 'swing kick' varia-

M1

JS1

M2

JS2

M3   JS3

M4   JS4

tion where all the drive across the circle is generated by the vigorous right leg action. Note how the 1kg discus is allowed to swing ahead of the body (M6), an action that

the discus being almost there in M6. Both have rangy positions — discus high — bodyweight over the right rear leg.

Photo 8 shows Schult holding his power

M5

M6   JS6

would spell disaster with the 2kg implement.

In photo 7 both athletes exhibit similar positions and Mikhalchenko has managed to manoeuvre the discus into position despite

position just prior to the left foot grounding, whereas Mikhalchenko has possibly driven the hip forward before grounding the front foot (somewhere between M7 and M8).

M7   JS7

M8   JS8

| M9 | JS9 | M10 | JS10 |

Schult drives the hip to the front and exhibits excellent left side block finishing with a fixed feet throw. Mikhalchenko drives the hips through on a bent right leg but does not establish a firm left side; the result is a 'back off' delivery and therefore less range at the end of the throw.

SKILL DRILLS

Half Turn Drill

Aim: to make the thrower feel the pivoting of the right foot as a direct result of the left leg drive.

Method: The starting position is with the right foot in the centre of the circle and the left foot in approximately the starting position for a half turn. The thrower should be fully wound up (Dr.1). The thrower then pushes off the left leg vigorously to initiate a fast right foot pivot so that the left foot is out of contact with the ground for as short a time as possible. Dr.2. demonstrates the mid-position. When the left foot hits the ground at the front, the right foot continues to pivot and push the hips into a throwing action (Dr.3).

Things to avoid

1. Initiating the drill with the shoulders.
2. Having the left foot land 'in the bucket' (i.e. too far round to the left) at the front of the circle.

| Dr.1 | Dr.2 | Dr.3 |

South African (or One and a Half Turn) Drill

Aim: to simulate the rhythm of a full throw without the complication of an added 90 degrees of movement.

Method: The thrower starts with his left foot at the back of the circle as for a normal turn, but 180 degrees round. The right foot is outside the circle, as far from the left foot as is comfortable, and the athlete is in a wound-up position (Dr.4). The thrower initiates the movement by moving his bodyweight over the left leg and then driving off it. The right leg is relaxed and follows an arc to the centre of the circle. The act of driving the left leg causes the discus to start moving upward and it should reach a high point at about 10 o'clock. This should coincide with the left foot touching the ground at the front of the circle. The thrower then pivots round the right foot and drives the legs vigorously to complete the throw (Dr.7).

Things to avoid

1. Initiating the movement with the shoulders.
2. Driving off the right foot at the rear of the circle.
3. Allowing the left foot to land 'in the bucket' at the front of the circle.

Dr.4

Dr.5

Dr.6

Dr.7

90 Degrees Drill

Aim: to ensure the athlete is on balance throughout the throw.

Method: The athlete starts at the back of the circle as for a full turn (Dr.8). He then performs a full turn, but touches the ground with his right foot every 90 degrees of rotation (Dr.9-11). When his right foot has landed in the centre of the circle, he then touches the ground with his left foot out to his left (Dr.12) midway in its move from the back of the circle (Dr.11) to the front (Dr.13).

Things to avoid

1. Falling from one static position to the next.

Dr.8   Dr.9   Dr.10

Dr.11   Dr.12   Dr.13

Back of the Circle Drill

Aim: to ensure that the athlete is on balance on entry.

Method: The thrower assumes a starting stance for a normal full turn (Dr.14). He then pivots over the left leg (Dr.15) through 360 degrees and returns to the starting position maintaining good balance.

Things to avoid

1. Initiating the movement with the shoulders.
2. Falling back into the starting position.

Dr.14

Dr.15

TRAINING FOR DISCUS

1992 Olympic Games

Average	Men	Women
Age	28 yrs 5 months	26 yrs 6 months
Weight	117 kgs	91 kgs
Height	1.94 m	1.80 m

The above statistics indicate that discus men and women are physically abnormal, but these figures do not reveal the power, the skill, the suppleness of the top class discus thrower. Great strength and size are not enough, and the coach and athlete must strive to achieve excellence in all facets of fitness. The five 'S's are often spoken of in athletics, and in the following text I will look at how these factors can be specifically developed for the discus thrower.

Skill

The old adage 'skill first, sweat second' holds good for the discus event. Specific skills should always be performed when the athlete is fresh and under no circumstances must the athlete be allowed to throw poorly due to fatigue.

Major technique changes should always be made during the early winter period and only small refinements should be considered close to or into the season.

The coach must always ensure that conditions for skill work are perfect. In the winter period this may necessitate moving indoors for net throwing. Exclusive net throwing may lead to technical problems since the athlete cannot see the effect on flight caused by his technique. It is always wise to ensure that the athlete throws outdoors at regular intervals.

The discus combines several different skills — turning balance at the back, turn across the circle, the final sling. It is sometimes beneficial to practise part skills and I have included these elsewhere in this booklet. However valuable part skills are, they must always be brought back into the whole and the closer the season comes, the more the whole skill must be the prime consideration. eg.

winter throws
session — 20 Half Turns
20 South African Turns
15 Full Throws

in season — 10 Half Turns
10 South African Turns
30 Full Throws

N.B.
1. Never work on more than one technical point at a time.
2. The coach must decide which point has priority.
3. Never treat the symptom when you can treat the cause.

Stamina

Although the discus throw is over in a split second, the thrower must have strength endurance for two vital areas of training:-
(a) *Throwing:* If skill is to be worked for, it can only be performed in a fatigue-free situation. The fitter the athlete, the more throws of quality he can execute. N.B. 'repetition is the mother of learning.'

(b) *Strength Training*. There is no easy way to build strength. Long hours are required in the strength room. The fitter the athlete, the more sets and repetitions he can perform.

The early part of the training year, ie. September/October, should be devoted to building up endurance which can consist of running, circuit training and high repetition weight-lifting. Once a satisfactory level has been attained, the athlete must ensure that this level is maintained by less arduous endurance routines fitted into his overall training programme.

Speed

Generally speed can be developed through sprinting, jumping and the explosive use of weight-lifting. For specific speed the athlete can use underweight throwing implements. A senior thrower can use a 1.75kg disc to great effect which will give him the experience of throwing distances that he aspires to. I would always use underweight implements as part of the session throughout the winter, eg. 30 throws full weight, 20 throws light, which would also give the added bonus of a change in the session just when the thrower is feeling bored or a little tired. The use of underweight implements is also useful at times when the coach believes a change would be beneficial, eg in mid-season when the athlete is a little stale and therefore would benefit from two weeks of total 1.75 kgs throwing. Coaches must be careful not to take this principle too far.

N.B.
1. Keep the implement within say 15 per cent of the competition weight. A senior athlete using a 1.5 kg would probably destroy his timing for the event.
2. Always ensure that full weight implement throwing is returned to in the period before an important competition.

Suppleness

For, the athlete to apply his force over as great a range as possible, he must improve his technique and ensure that his mobility is such that he can assume rangy positions.

It is necessary to perform general mobility every day if possible and a convenient way of achieving this is for the athlete to perform mobility in his warm-up for training.

It is advisable to perform some specific mobility sessions in order to increase rather than to maintain mobility. The athlete may have concentrated sessions in early winter to increase his range and thereafter try to maintain this new found mobility.

As with most aspects of fitness, mobility is specific and the ability to touch your toes may not help you to assume a powerful, rangy throwing position. Therefore the athlete should look at the discus action and try to design simulated discus mobility exercises.

The exercises illustrated are examples of mobility exercises related to the discus action.

Mobility Exercises

Torso

Shoulders

Strength

To throw the discus a long way an athlete must be strong. This apparently simple statement does not reveal the complexity of strength training, ie. what kind of strength? with what? when? how much?

The young athlete should go through a long period of conditioning before commencing weight-lifting. This would include circuit training, bodyweight exercises and multigym exercises which may very well take him into his late teens. To commence lifting heavy weights at too young an age may lead to injuries, especially when over-loading the spine and knee areas before final ossification.

The lifting of weights is the tried and tested and almost certainly the best method of gaining gross strength for throwing. The schedule will revolve around basic lifts:-

Pulling
— Clean (St. 1–3) or Snatching.
Pushing
— Bench Press (St. 4 & 5), Pressing.
Squatting
— Back Squat, Front Squat, Jump Squat etc. (St. 6 & 7)

The Clean

start	St.1	mid-point	St.2	receiving position	St.3

Bench Press

start & finish   St.4

mid-point   St.5

The Back Squat

start & finish   St.6

mid-point   St.7

Added to these will be event specific lifts such as Bent Arm Flys (St. 8 & 9) and assistance exercises such as Curls and Tricep Extensions. It is of vital importance not to neglect the torso/trunk region and Sit-ups, Hyper-extensions, Side-bends must always feature prominently in the schedule.

A critical decision in the formulation of a weights schedule is how many repetitions of each exercise must be performed. Performing sets of 3 to 8 reps will be the basic routine for the discus thrower, although he may at

Bent-arm Fly

start & finish   St.8   mid-point   St.9

certain times of the year lift in singles for gross strength or train at high repetitions for strength endurance. An example of how the choice of repetition system changes can be seen as follows:-

October	— sets of 10
November/December	— sets of 8
January/March	— sets of 5
April	— singles
May onwards	— 5 reps (fast)

(suitable for a young athlete of inter-mediate development)

Basic Strength Exercises

The Squat

Gains in gross strength are easily attained, but the activity of discus throwing does not always correlate highly with increases in gross strength. It is the amount of elastic (explosive) strength present that dictates the distance thrown.

Elastic (explosive) strength is obtained via:-
(a) Lifting weights in an explosive manner, eg 5 repetitions in six seconds.
(b) Jumping — eg standing long jump, bounding, depth jumping etc. Be careful since heavy throwers may be susceptible to injury when performing high repetitions or bounding.
(c) Throwing heavy weights — be careful not to disturb the timing of the throw. It might be worthwhile to restrict heavy throwing to the standing position only.

In the period immediately prior to competition (final 4-6 weeks) this linking of gross and elastic strength is vital and a session such as follows may lead to improvement:
1. Bench Press — 4 sets of 5 reps (fast) super-setted with medicine ball throw — 6 reps.
2. Bench Squats — 4 sets of 6 reps (fast) super-setted with vertical jump (no weights).
3. Clean — 4 sets of 4 reps (fast) super-setted with overhead medicine ball throw.

N.B. Super-set: Two exercises performed one after another without rest, to form one set.

Exercises for torso strength and conditioning

In the competitive season the overall volume of strength training must be reduced to allow quality work in other areas to take place. It is important to ensure that strength levels are kept high during the season and that contact must be kept with weights even during the long hot summer.

The strength assistance exercises illustrated are specifically for strengthening the torso muscles, frequently the most neglected part of the athlete's body.

The strength training area is dealt with in detail in the B.A.F. booklet 'Strength Training'.

Maintaining the Balance

Having noted how important it is to include all aspects of fitness in the discus thrower's schedule, the problem for the coach is *how much* and *when*. The schedule of an athlete is not static. It constantly changes to reflect the time of year, the fitness of the athlete and the needs of the athlete. Advanced athletes will operate to a schedule that needs finer tuning than that of a novice.

A. A novice (14 year old) schedule would be less complex, eg:

		Winter		Summer
Sun	(1)	Technique work × 20 throws	(i)	Technique work × 30 throws
	(ii)	Second event work	(ii)	Sprinting & other events
Mon		———		———
Tues	(i)	Mobility session	(i)	Throwing — 20 throws
	(ii)	Circuit training	(ii)	Jumping
Wed		———		———
Thurs	(i)	Basic technique work	(i)	Throwing — 20 throwa
	(ii)	Circuit training	(ii)	Hurdling etc.
Fri		———		———
Sat		———		Competition — several events

B. Sample schedule for 18 year old of several years' experience

	Strength	Specific strength	Elastic strength	Endurance	Technique	Rest days
Sept/Oct. (6 wks.)	general exercises 3 sets of 10 reps × 3/wk.	medicine ball work — high reps × 1/wk	—	4,000m. steady run cycling etc circuits × 3/wk.	× 1 session	2
Nov/Dec	Basic lifts. 4 sets 6 reps × 3/wk.	med. ball work × 1/wk.	Bounding 8 sets of 3 bunnies 60m fast strides × 2/wk	4,000m steady run × 1/wk.	outdoor session × 1/wk. net throwing × 1/wk.	2
Jan/March	Basic lifts 4 × 5 reps and pyramid work × 3/wk.	med. ball work × 1/wk. shot thrown discus style × 1/wk.	Bounding 1 × wk. 40m sprints × 5 × 1/wk.	4,000m steady run × 1/wk.	outdoor × 2/wk. net throwing × 1/wk.	2
April/May	as Jan/Mar. reduced volume × 3/wk.	as Jan/Mar.	Bounding 1/wk. 40m sprints × 5 × 2/wk.	—	outdoor × 3/wk.	1
June/ August	moderate poundages × 1/wk.	1/wk.	as above	—	outdoor × 5/wk.	1

Added to the above would of course be the athlete's physical education programme which would almost certainly provide him with an endurance background. For the novice the schedule should be:-

(a) simple
(b) not too event specific
(c) not too demanding on time or energy output.

Advanced

It is now important that the coach looks at the year in detail and phases the programme. The division of the athletic year into separate training periods is called PERIODISATION.

Single Periodised Year:

months	Nov	Dec	Jan	Feb	Mar	Apr	May	Jun	Jul	Aug	Sep	Oct
phases		1				2		3	4		5	6
periods	preparation						competition					transition

Double Periodised Year:

months	Nov	Dec	Jan	Feb	Mar	Apr	May	Jun	Jul	Aug	Sep	Oct
phases	1_1		2_1		3_1	1_2		2_2	3_2	4	5	6
periods	preparation			competition		preparation			competition			transition

The phasing-periodising of the year against the months indicated is a suggestion for illustration. Commencement of the "year" will vary according to individual circumstances and requirements.

The aim of periodisation is to ensure that a firm base or foundation is established before more specific work is attempted. The foundation or preparation phases consist of high volume/low intensity general work, which gradually changes to the competitive phase when the volume is low and the intensity high. It is important not to have sudden changes, but to ensure that each phase blends into the next.

To plan the training year, the coach should follow several simple planning steps which are:-

1) Decide which competitions are important, since this will naturally form the competitive phase.
2) Working back through the year, decide how to divide the year into preparation, competitive and transition phases.
3) Decide the needs of the particular athlete and then sub-divide each phase with the aspects of fitness required; all will be included, but with varying importance depending upon the phase, eg. in the preparation phase, strength is very important and takes a lot of the time, whereas in the competitive phase it becomes far less important.
4) Decide which methods are to be used to develop the physical qualities in each phase.
5) The athlete's personal commitment and time available will have to be assessed.
6) Formulate the training schedule.

Table B outlines an example of a periodised year of a thrower of Great Britain International standard.

THE ADVANCED THROWER — AN OUTLINE SCHEDULE

TABLE B

PHASES	1¹ (Nov–Dec)	2¹ (Jan)	3¹ (Feb–mid-March)	1² (Mid-March–April)	2² (May)
PERIODS	PREPARATION		COMP	PREPARATION	
STRENGTH	Many exercises — basically 3 sets of 10 reps, moving to 4 sets of 8 reps by end of phase. (3×/wk.)	Mixture of 75%–85% work, moving to 85%–95% work; major muscle group work (×3–5/wk.)	Lower volume — explosive work, eg. 5 reps in 6 secs. (×3/wk.)	75%–85% of work (×3/wk.)	85%–95% work — lower volume near end of phase. (×3–4/wk.)
EXPLOSIVE/ ELASTIC STRENGTH	Medicine ball work — high reps, many exercises. (2×/wk.)	Bounding — 6–8 foot contacts (×2/wk.) Medicine ball work — 10 reps, heavy ball (×1/wk.)	Quality bounding, 2/3 foot contacts (×2/wk.) (early part)	Bounding — 6 foot contacts ×1/wk. Medicine ball work — 8 reps (×1/wk.)	Bounding — 3 foot contacts (×2/wk.)
SPECIFIC STRENGTH		Heavy shot work, 8–9 kg standing puts (×2/wk.)		Heavy shot work as for phase 2.	—
TECHNIQUE	Major skill changes, light discus (eg. 1.75 kg men) (2×/wk.)	Discus of variable weights ±10% of comp. weight (×3/wk.)	Comp. work, standard & light (1.9) discus (×4/wk.)	Comp. work — variable weights ±10% (×4/wk.)	Comp. work — standard & light (1.9) discus (×5/wk.)
RUNS	4000m jog (×1/wk.) 6×100m strides (×2/wk.)	6×100m (×1/wk.) 6×30 m (indoors) (×1/wk.)	4×30 — indoor — timed (×1/wk.)	4×150m easy strides. (×1/wk.)	6×30 m (×1/wk.) 4×60 m (×1/wk.)
MOBILITY	Specific session (×2/wk.) aiming to improve weak spots + normal everyday session.	Everyday regime, eg. incorporated in warm-up.			

Continued overleaf

TABLE B – continued

PHASES PERIODS	3² (June)	4 (July) COMPETITION	5 (Aug–Sept) COMPETITION	6 (Oct) TRANSITION
STRENGTH	Explosive work — 5 reps/6 secs sandwiched (super-setted) with stretch reflex work. ($\times 3$/wk.)	Low volume explosive work ($\times 3$/wk.)	as 3b.	(at the end of the competitive season) Three weeks of active rest, e.g. swimming, squash, jogging, etc.
EXPLOSIVE/ ELASTIC STRENGTH	Low volume/high quality 1–2 foot contact ($\times 2$/wk.)	Bounding — 3 foot contacts ($\times 1$/wk.)	as 3b.	
SPECIFIC STRENGTH	—	—	—	
TECHNIQUE	Comp. weight discus work ($\times 5$/wk.)	1.9 kg discus work — quality ($\times 3$/wk.)	repeat 3²	
RUNS	$4 \times 30+$ m timed ($\times 1$/wk.)	4×60 m fast strides ($\times 2$/wk.)		
MOBILITY	Everyday regime eg. incorporated in warm-up			

C. A World Class Thrower

Finally I have reprinted the schedule of former World Champion Imrich Bugar to show the depth and complexity of a world class discus thrower's training. Before going into the details of the schedule, I have given a table showing exactly how Bugar built up year by year the intensity of his training. However the enthusiastic discus thrower should not be tempted to emulate at once Bugar's eventual volume of training.

Age	20	21	22	23	24	25	26	27
training days	163	158	222	213	205	236	216	249
sessions	177	187	258	278	250	319	267	323
tons lifted	738	1029	1491	1503	1498	1861	1434	1646
throwa	2620	1890	1640	2645	2523	2729	2180	2195
jumps	2960	4210	5770	4400	4830	6270	5110	5790
stomach/back repetitions	3020	3990	4770	4260	2520	5715	6130	6220
competitions	27	16	25	26	25	26	22	25
weight (av) kgs	104	108	108	113	115	117	118	120
Tests	75	76	77	78	79	80	81	82
20 m Sprint	3.10	3.10	3.10	3.10	3.00	3.00	3.05	3.05
T. Jump	9.00	9.20	9.35	9.23	9.14	9.20	9.38	9.20
Snatch	95	110	120	135	135	140	135	140
Bench press	115	130	145	170	170	190	180	200
Clean	120	140	145	170	170	175	170	180
Squat	170	210	200	250	240	240	220	240
5 kg Shot (discus style)	20.97	23.10	23.70	24.06	25.95	27.00	26.11	27.37
7.25 kg shot overhead	—	—	—	—	20.16	22.10	20.70	21.50
4 kg Shot with turn, discus style.	—	—	—	—	37.45	37.20	37.82	37.65
Performance	53.88	57.52	62.54	65.96	64.98	66.38	67.48	68.60

Training carried out by Imrich Bugar

Planned on basis of previous year's experience. Divided into 4 phases:-

1) recovery	1–2 cycles	Sept./Oct.
2) training 1	3	Nov./Feb.
3) training 2	3	March/April
4) competition	5	May onwards

Recovery period includes little actual training — warm-ups and light activities are important in this phase.

Training phase 1

Aims
— development of general and event strength for maximum stamina.
— leg power.
— correct technique.

Training phase 2

Aims
— strength development for competition.

— leg power and various running exercises for increasing speed.
— intensive technique development.

Competition phase

— continuing attention to technique.
— maintenance of peak condition.

A closer look at the seasons

Recovery:
'Rehabilitation', swimming, games, outdoor training and recovery from physical injuries and psychological stress of competition season.

Training 1:
Starts with a light training session/day increasing gradually until there are double sessions 2-3 days/week. General conditioning and strength training stressed — 70-80% of training time. Micro-cycles repeated 6-8 times. Later one third strength training aims at quality 80-90% level, microcycle repeat 3-5 times. Tests before each training cycle.

Training 2:
Stress on speed and running. Most specialist strength sessions use discus throwing as their basis, with attention to technique. Intensity 90-100% in training during this period.
Strength training — 2/3 quality orientated
                  1/3 volume orientated.
   Tests used throughout period, final control test at end of training 2 when there are 3-5 double session days.

Competition:
In principle session/day ie. training volume decreases, but timing and importance of competition influences this. Special strength training with discus, close observation of technique. 2-3 weights sessions/week — *quality*. Also used: jumps and sprints.

Sample weeks

Training Phase I

Monday Cycle 1

30 min. warm-up
50 jumps
100 varied medicine ball throws
rope climbing 2 x 4m
back & stomach muscles 3 x 20
massage & sauna

Monday Cycle 2

Warm-up and bar exercises 6x6x60kg.
strength training — 20 tons
snatch 5x6x80kg.
squat 6x6x130kg.
clean 2x6x90/2x5x100/2x3x110/2x6x90
bench, wide grip:-
      2x6x90/2x6x100/2x4x110/2x6x90
body twists, standing:-
      5x10x60

Tuesday

30 min. warm-up
5 sprints
5 starts + 20m
30 x 4kg shot, discus style
20 x 5kg weight discus style
5 x standing long jumps
1200m jogging

Wednesday

Weights — 25 tons.
Warm-up 6x6x60kg
snatch 1x6x80/2x5x90/2x4x95/2x2x100
clean 2x6x90/2x5x100/2x4x110/2x2x120
bench 2x6x90/2x6x100/2x4x110/2x2x120
squat 1x6x100/2x5x120/2x5x140/
      2x5x150/2x4x160
twists, sitting 6x6x60
70 medicine ball throws
back & stomach muscles 3x20/sauna.

Thursday

Warm-up 30 mins.
Exercises with 10kg weight disc:-
5x10x i) arms out to side, to front.
      ii) hands vertical stretching
      iii) swings of arms.
Clean 5x10x60
20 mins swimming.

Friday Cycle 1

20 min warm-up
3 sprints
5 starts
30 x 4kg shot throws
20 x 5kg weight throws
100 jumps (stairs)
Back & stomach exercises 3x20

Friday Cycle 2

Strength training as Monday in the afternoon.

Saturday

30 min warm-up
Circuit x 3/5 min recovery:
skipping
feet together jumping
rope climbing
stomach muscles x 30
back muscles x 30
body twists 10 x 60kg.
30 mins games
20 mins swimming

Sunday

Free

Training Phase 11 (April in Italy)
Monday Cycle 1

20 min warm-up

35 discus throws/technique
weights: 3 x snatch/squat/twists 12 tons.
1000m jogging

Cycle 2

25 throws — technique
weights: 5 x 150 bench; clean; 8 tons.
exercises — 15 mins.
(note — imprecise details of weights programme)

Tuesday

15 mins warm-up
10 x 5kg shot throws (discus technique)
20 x 4kg weight-lifting disc throws, discus style.
50 various throws with weights.
5 x 20 sprints from blocks.
warm-down, 1000m jogging.

Wednesday Cycle 1

Warm-up
50 x discus throws
800m jogging

Wednesday Cycle 2

weights: 5 x squat/snatch/bench/twists — 21 tons.
use of exercise machines
ball games, eg. football.

Thursday Cycle 1

Warm-up
30 throws/technique
10 x 4kg shot throws, discus style.
20 mins exercises

Thursday Cycle 2

Warm-up
25 throws/technique
50 x 15kg medicine ball throws.
50 jumps
2000m jogging & massage.

Friday Cycle 1

Warm-up
40 throws
6 tons weights
20 mins stretching

Friday Cycle 2

30 throws
13 tons weights — snatch/bench/30 mins
exercises
sauna.

Saturday, Cycle 1

Light weights warm-up
Special strength:-
— step-ups onto bench, arms outstretched
  with 15kg.
— squat jumps onto bench, 80kg on bar.
— cleans, 60kg
— twists, 60kg on bar.
— ditto, 20kg weight, arms outstretched.
— 1000m jogging.

Saturday Cycle 2

Jogging
30 throws
50 x 15kg medicine ball
jogging.

Sunday

— active recovery — football.

Programme Pre-Czechoslovakian Record Throw

Day 1
Warm-up 20 mins; 30 technique throws; 5 x
40m knee-lift running; 5 sprints, accelerating
to maximum; steam bath etc.

Day 2
Warm-up & light weights; weights — 3 exercises at maximum efficiency; bench 3 x 180,
squat 5 x 200, snatch 2 x 130, 5 x 1 x 140.
Special strength — 2 exercises: lying on
bench 5 x 10 x 15, squat jumps onto bench 5
x 6 x 60; 1000m jogging; massage & sauna.

Day 3
Jogging & warm-up 20 mins.
  20 throws/technique; 10 x 4kg shot
throws; 60 jumps/ankles; 3 sprints; light
running.

Day 4
Warm-up exercises; weights — 2 exercises;
clean 1 x 5 x 140, 1 x 4 x 160; 1 x 2 x 180;
squat 1 x 5 x 160; 1 x 4 x 150; 1 x 3 x 200.
800m jogging; steam bath etc.

Day 5
Warm-up: 15 throws, alternate throws at
maximum efficiency: exercises.

Day 6
15 min. warm-up: 20 x 7.25kg shot throws,
various ankle exercises 3 x 20: jogging.

Day 7
Competition — *RECORD* 68.60m!

TESTS AND MEASUREMENTS
Evaluating your thrower

The only true test or measurement is the
event and no other activity correlates totally
with discus throwing — but this is not a
reason to disregard measurements from
other tests. Such tests can provide the athlete
with motivation and the coach with informa-

tion relating to the state of fitness of his/her athlete at any time of the year. The following statistics of Glen Smith (British junior record holder) show how many simple ways there are to evaluate one's progress:-

Height: 6'2½"
Age: 19
30 m Sprint: 3.68 s
Three bounds: 9.86 m
Overhead shot (6.25 kg) 19.02 m
Power clean: 150 kg
Parallel back squat: 252½ kg
Bench press: 152½ kg
1½ kg discus throw: 63.16 m
1 kg discus throw: 72.20 m
Vertical jump: 75 cms
Bench press — 5 reps in 5 secs: 92½ kg

Weight: 100 kg
Best performance: 55.10 m (2 kg)
Standing long jump: 3.12 m
Overhead shot (7.26 kg): 17.89 m
Five bounds: 15.10 m
Snatch: 107½ kg
Front squat: 212½ kg
Bench press (pause): 135 kg
1.75 kg discus: 60.76 m
2 kg discus throw (left hand): 45.90 m

No test is a substitute for the event itself and often the correlation is a poor one. The most popular battery of tests currently used in the UK is the 'Test Quadrathlon'. Detailed scoring tables are given in Table A with the following target scores being the incentive:-

	Elite	International	Regional	Club
Men	325+	290	265	240
Women	265	240	225	200

TEST QUADRATHLON
How it Works
Standing Long Jump

Place feet over the edge of the sandpit. The athlete crouches, leans forward, swings his arms backwards, then jumps horizontally as far as possible, jumping from both feet into a sandpit (which should be level with take-off). Measure (metric) to the nearest point of contact.

N.B. The start of the jump must be from a static position.

Three Jumps

Start with the feet comfortably apart with toes just behind the take-off mark. The

athlete takes three *continuous* two-footed bounds into the sandpit (level with take-off). *N.B.* Spikes allowed. Static start — feet must be parallel on each jump phase.

30 Metre Sprint

On the command the athlete moves to the set position. On the start signal he sprints from a *stationary* set position as fast as possible to the finish line. The time-keeper stands at the finish and times the run from the moment that the runner's foot contacts the ground on the first running stride to the moment when the runner's torso crosses the line. Spikes allowed. Hand timed.

Overhead Shot Throw

The athlete stands on the shot stopboard, facing away from the landing area, with his feet a comfortable distance apart. The shot is held cupped in both hands. He crouches, lowering the shot between his legs, then drives upwards to cast the shot back over his head. There is no penalty for following through, but the thrower must land feet first and remain upright. Measurements (to the nearest cm) are taken from the inside of the stopboard. Implements are as per BAF age group. Please watch the safety aspect.

Practical uses

Both athlete and coach can use the Quadrathlon to gauge whether he/she is becoming more powerful, and the benefits are threefold:
1) If the athlete's score increases, then his power has increased.
2) Weaknesses can be identified if the athlete 'underscores' and these areas can be worked on.
3) Motivational help during the long winter months.

TEST QUADRATHLON TABLES (1992)

Points	3 Jumps	S.L.J	30 m	O.H. Shot	Points	3 Jumps	S.L.J.	30 m	O.H. Shot
1	3.00	1.00	5.80	4.00	51	7.04	2.36	4.38	12.58
2	3.08	1.02	5.77	4.17	52	7.12	2.39	4.35	12.75
3	3.16	1.05	5.74	4.34	53	7.20	2.41	4.33	12.92
4	3.24	1.08	5.71	4.51	54	7.28	2.44	4.30	13.10
5	3.32	1.10	5.68	4.68	55	7.36	2.47	4.27	13.27
6	3.40	1.13	5.66	4.85	56	7.44	2.50	4.24	13.44
7	3.48	1.16	5.63	5.03	57	7.52	2.52	4.21	13.61
8	3.56	1.19	5.60	5.20	58	7.60	2.55	4.18	13.78
9	3.64	1.21	5.57	5.37	59	7.68	2.58	4.16	13.95
10	3.72	1.24	5.54	5.54	60	7.76	2.60	4.13	14.13
11	3.80	1.27	5.51	5.71	61	7.84	2.63	4.10	14.30
12	3.88	1.30	5.49	5.88	62	7.92	2.66	4.07	14.47
13	3.96	1.32	5.46	6.06	63	8.01	2.69	4.04	14.64
14	4.05	1.35	5.43	6.23	64	8.09	2.71	4.02	14.81
15	4.13	1.38	5.40	6.40	65	8.17	2.74	3.99	14.98
16	4.21	1.40	5.37	6.57	66	8.25	2.77	3.96	15.16
17	4.29	1.43	5.34	6.74	67	8.33	2.80	3.93	15.33
18	4.37	1.46	5.32	6.91	68	8.41	2.82	3.90	15.50
19	4.45	1.49	5.29	7.09	69	8.49	2.85	3.87	15.67
20	4.53	1.51	5.26	7.26	70	8.57	2.88	3.85	15.84
21	4.61	1.54	5.23	7.43	71	8.65	2.90	3.82	16.02
22	4.69	1.57	5.20	7.60	72	8.73	2.93	3.79	16.19
23	4.77	1.60	5.17	7.77	73	8.81	2.96	3.76	16.36
24	4.85	1.62	5.15	7.94	74	8.89	2.99	3.73	16.53
25	4.93	1.65	5.12	8.12	75	8.97	3.01	3.70	16.70
26	5.02	1.68	5.09	8.29	76	9.06	3.04	3.68	16.87
27	5.10	1.70	5.06	8.46	77	9.14	3.07	3.65	17.05
28	5.18	1.73	5.03	8.63	78	9.22	3.10	3.62	17.22
29	5.26	1.76	5.01	8.80	79	9.30	3.12	3.59	17.39
30	5.34	1.79	4.98	8.97	80	9.38	3.15	3.56	17.56
31	5.42	1.81	4.95	9.15	81	9.46	3.18	3.53	17.73
32	5.50	1.84	4.92	9.32	82	9.54	3.20	3.51	17.90
33	5.58	1.87	4.89	9.49	83	9.62	3.23	3.48	18.03
34	5.66	1.90	4.86	9.66	84	9.70	3.26	3.45	18.23
35	5.74	1.92	4.84	9.83	85	9.78	3.29	3.42	18.42
36	5.82	1.95	4.81	10.01	86	9.86	3.31	3.39	18.59
37	5.90	1.98	4.78	10.18	87	9.94	3.34	3.36	18.76
38	5.98	2.00	4.75	10.35	88	10.03	3.37	3.34	18.93
39	6.07	2.03	4.72	10.52	89	10.11	3.40	3.31	19.11
40	6.15	2.06	4.69	10.69	90	10.19	3.42	3.28	19.28
41	6.23	2.09	4.67	10.86	91	10.27	3.45	3.25	19.45
42	6.31	2.11	4.64	11.04	92	10.35	3.48	3.22	19.62
43	6.39	2.14	4.61	11.21	93	10.43	3.50	3.20	19.79
44	6.47	2.17	4.58	11.38	94	10.51	3.53	3.18	19.96
45	6.55	2.20	4.55	11.55	95	10.59	3.56	3.15	20.14
46	6.63	2.22	4.52	11.72	96	10.67	3.59	3.12	20.31
47	6.71	2.25	4.50	11.89	97	10.75	3.61	3.09	20.48
48	6.79	2.28	4.47	12.07	98	10.83	3.64	3.06	20.65
49	6.87	2.30	4.44	12.24	99	10.91	3.67	3.03	20.82
50	6.95	2.33	4.41	12.41	100	11.00	3.70	3.01	21.00

Additional Points: 3 Jumps: 1 Point for each 8 cms above 11.00.   30 m 1 point for each 0.03 below 3.01
S.L.J.: 1 Point for each 3 cm above 3.70   O.H. Shot: 1 point for each 7 cm above 21.00

51

FURTHER READING

Teaching Discus

How To Teach The Throws — M. F. Jones (BAF)
But First — F. W. Dick (BAF)
Fundamentals of Track & Field — G. A. Carr (Leisure Press Canada)

Discus Technique

Throwing — M. F. Jones (Crowood Press)
Athletes in Action — A. H. Payne (IAAF)
The Throws — J. Jarver (Track & Field News Press USA)
Track & Field Coaching Manual — V. Gambetta (TAC USA)
The Throws Manual — K. McGill & G. D. Dunn (Track & Field News Press USA)

Strength Training

Strength Training — M. F. Jones (BAF)
Weight Lifting — J. Lear (A. & C. Black)
Weight Training and Lifting — J. Lear (A. & C. Black)
The Powerlifters Manual — J. Lear (EP Pub. Ltd)
Powerlifting — F. C. Hatfield (Contemporary Books USA)
Weight Training for Sport — B. & G. Tancred (Hodder & Stoughton)
Designing Resistance Training Programs — S. J. Fleck (Human Kinetics USA)
Strength & Power in Sport — P. V. Komi (Blackwell Scientific Publications)
Strength Training for Coaches — B. Pauletto (Leisure Press USA)

Training Theory

The Science of Track & Field Athletics — H. & R. Payne (Pelham Books)
Sports Training Principles — F. W. Dick (A. & C. Black London)
Training Theory — F. W. Dick (BAF)
Athletic Ability & The Anatomy of Motion — R. Wirhead (Wolfe Medical Pub. Ltd)

First published 1950 (H.A.L. Chapman)
Reprinted   1951, 1955
Second Edition   1957 (John Le Masurier)
Reprinted   1959, 1960, 1962, 1964
Third Edition   1967 (John Le Masurier)
Reprinted   1972
Fourth Edition   1976 (Wilf Paish)
Fifth Edition   1985 (Max Jones)
This Edition   1993 (Max Jones)

ISBN 0 85134 114 4   3M/40M/04.93

© British Athletic Federation
225a Bristol Road,
Birmingham B5 7UB

Typeset in Times by BPCC Whitefriars Ltd
and printed & bound in England by BPCC
Wheatons on 115 gsm Fineblade Cartridge.

DISCUS
THROWING

Max Jones
(B.A.F. National Coach)